W9-AAC-916

About Crustaceans

For the One who created crustaceans.

—Genesis 1:25

Ω

Published by
PEACHTREE PUBLISHERS
1700 Chattahoochee Avenue
Atlanta, Georgia 30318-2112
www.peachtree-online.com

Text © 2004 by Cathryn P. Sill
Illustrations © 2004 by John C. Sill

Illustrations created in watercolor on archival quality 100% rag watercolor paper
Text and titles set in Novarese from Adobe Systems

Printed in April 2012 by Imago in Singapore
10 9 8 7 6 5 4 3 (hardcover)
10 9 8 7 6 5 4 3 2 (trade paperback)

Library of Congress Cataloging-in-Publication Data

Sill, Cathryn P., 1953-
      About crustaceans / written by Cathryn Sill ; illustrated by John Sill.
            p. cm--1st ed.
Summary: Describes the anatomy, behavior, and habitat of various crustaceans, including the lobster, crab, and shrimp.
         ISBN 13: 978-1-56145-301-6 / ISBN 10: 1-56145-301-3 (hardcover)
         ISBN 13: 978-1-56145-405-1 / ISBN 10: 1-56145-405-2 (trade paperback)
1. Crustacea--Juvenile literature. [1. Crustaceans.] I. Sill, John, ill. II. Title.
QL437.2.S56 2004
595.3--dc22
                  2003016838

About Crustaceans

A Guide for Children

Cathryn Sill

Illustrated by John Sill

Ω

PEACHTREE

ATLANTA

Crustaceans have a hard shell on the outside of their bodies.

PLATE 1
California Rock Lobster

(also shown: Señorita)

The hard shell protects the soft body
of the crustacean.

When a crustacean outgrows its shell, it sheds the old shell and grows a new one.

PLATE 3
Northern Lobster

Crustaceans feel, smell, and taste
with their antennae.

Some crustaceans' eyes are on stalks. This makes it easier for them to look around.

Most crustaceans have several pairs of legs. Some use them to walk. Others use them to swim or dig.

PLATE 6
Land Hermit Crab, Lady Crab,
Sand Fiddler

Legs with pincers can be used for protection as well as for gathering food.

Some crustaceans can regrow a leg that has been broken or bitten off by an enemy.

Many crustaceans are predators—they hunt and eat other animals.

Some are scavengers, eating dead plants and animals.

PLATE 10
Ghost Crab

Most crustaceans live in the oceans.

Some live in streams, ponds, and lakes.

A few live on land.

PLATE 13
Pill Bug

Crustaceans provide food for many animals and people.

PLATE 14
Krill

(*also shown: Blue Whale and Yellowfin Tuna*)

Crustaceans are an important part of our world.

PLATE 15
White Shrimp
(*also shown: Snowy Egret*)

Afterword

PLATE 1

Crustaceans are arthropods—animals with distinctly divided body parts, jointed legs, and a hard outer covering called an exoskeleton. They include lobsters, shrimp, crabs, barnacles, pill bugs, and many other less familiar species. California Rock Lobsters (16 inches long*) do not have large pincers like some other crustaceans, but their shells have strong spines that protect them from predators. They live in rocky tide pools and below the low-tide line.

PLATE 2

The hard shell of crustaceans acts like armor, which makes it difficult for other animals to eat them. The colorful shells of Calico Crabs (2 5/8 inches wide) have bright patches that help them blend in with their surroundings. Calico Crabs live on sandy bottoms in bays and the open ocean. They are an important source of food for some endangered sea turtles.

PLATE 3

When a crustacean sheds its exoskeleton, the process is called molting. Younger crustaceans molt more often because they grow faster. Many crustaceans eat the shed exoskeleton to get calcium to make their new shell stronger. The period right after molting is a dangerous time for crustaceans. The new shells are soft and offer little protection until they harden. Northern Lobsters (34 inches long) can weigh up to 45 pounds. Lobsters this size grow slowly and may molt less than once a year. Northern Lobsters live on rocky ocean bottoms.

* Sizes vary. All measurements in the Afterword are approximate, and are for adults.

PLATE 4

Sense organs called antennae help crustaceans know about their environment. Some crustaceans have stubby antennae. Others like the Red-lined Cleaning Shrimp (2 3/4 inches long) have long thin ones. Their antennae, which bend over their backs and beyond their tails, can warn them of danger approaching from the rear. Cleaning shrimp get their name from their habit of cleaning parasites and diseased tissue from the skin and mouth of fishes. Red-lined Cleaning Shrimp live on rocks, jetties, and coral reefs.

PLATE 5

The well-developed stalked eyes of Mantis Shrimp (10 inches long) allow them to spot their prey easily and help make them successful predators. Mantis Shrimp also have a very sharp claw called a "jackknife claw" that can slice another shrimp in two. This claw can cause serious injury to people who try to catch them. Mantis Shrimp dig burrows on the ocean bottom to live in.

PLATE 6

Land Hermit Crabs (1 1/2 inches long) do not have a protective shell over their abdomen, so they live in empty shells of other mollusks. Their first pair of walking legs has rounded pincers that help them grasp food as well as move about.

Lady Crabs' (3 inches wide) last pair of legs is flattened to enable them to swim.

Sand Fiddlers (1 1/2 inches wide) use their legs to dig burrows. They retreat to the burrows when the tide is high and plug the entrance with wet sand or mud.

PLATE 7

The large claws of some crustaceans make them look threatening and make them difficult for a predator to catch. Blue Crabs (9 1/4 inches wide) are fast and agile. They snap their pincers aggressively when caught or threatened. Blue Crabs live in brackish waters (where salt water mixes with fresh water) and shallow ocean waters.

PLATE 8

Some crustaceans are able to regrow claws lost in accidents or encounters with predators. This regrowth is called regeneration. Stone Crabs (4 5/8 inches wide) are a source of crab claws, a popular seafood dish. In many places, people are not allowed to keep the Stone Crabs they catch. They can break off the large pincer and release the crab so it can grow a new one. It usually takes two or more molts for a new leg to grow.

PLATE 9

Green Crabs (3 inches wide) sometimes will position themselves close to schools of small fish that swim near the bottom of the ocean. The crabs are able to lash out quickly with their pincers and catch fish to eat. Green Crabs were introduced to North America from Europe. Often, introduced species are a threat to native animals and plants. The invasion of the aggressive Green Crab is a problem along both United States coasts. They eat some native animals and eat the food of others.

PLATE 10

Ghost Crabs (2 inches wide) scavenge mostly in the evening on bits of plant and animal debris that have been washed up by the surf. They live on beaches and dig burrows in the drier sand above the high-tide line. These crustaceans are named Ghost Crabs because their sandy color and quickness make them seem to appear and disappear suddenly into their surroundings.

PLATE 11

Common Goose Barnacles (6 inches long) are oceanic crustaceans that often wash ashore along both North American coasts. They attach themselves to floating objects by a long rubbery stalk that resembles a goose's neck. Objects that have been floating in the ocean for a long time may be covered with thousands of barnacles.

PLATE 12

Crayfish (size varies, but usually 3 inches long) are found mostly in fresh water. Many live under rocks in streams and ponds. There are also some semiaquatic forms that burrow in mud to get water. The burrow may be away from a stream, but it is deep enough for the bottom to fill with water. Crayfish are also called crawfish or crawdads.

PLATE 13

Even though they live on land, Pill Bugs (less than 1/2 inch long) must live in damp places to keep from drying out. Pill Bugs are active at night, and during the day they hide under logs, rocks, or leaf piles. They eat mostly dead plants and other decaying material. Pill Bugs roll into tight little balls when threatened. Another common name for these small terrestrial crustaceans is "roly-poly."

PLATE 14

Krill (2 inches long) are small shrimplike crustaceans that congregate by the millions in cold ocean waters. They provide food for many animals, including the Blue Whale (100 feet long), the largest animal that has ever lived. This whale can eat up to 4 tons of krill a day. Krill are also a vital food source for penguins, seals, and large fish such as basking sharks.

PLATE 15

Crustaceans are a critical part of many food chains. Environmental threats—such as wetland destruction and pollution—endanger not only crustaceans, but also the other animals that feed on them. Commercial fishing for several types of crustaceans is a major industry, providing income as well as a valuable food source for many people. White Shrimp (8 inches long) are an important commercial species.

ISBN 978-1-56145-234-7 HC
ISBN 978-1-56145-312-2 PB

ISBN 978-1-56145-038-1 HC
ISBN 978-1-56145-364-1 PB

ISBN 978-1-56145-028-2 HC
ISBN 978-1-56145-147-0 PB

ISBN 978-1-56145-301-6 HC
ISBN 978-1-56145-405-1 PB

ISBN 978-1-56145-256-9 HC
ISBN 978-1-56145-335-1 PB

ISBN 978-1-56145-207-1 HC
ISBN 978-1-56145-232-3 PB

ISBN 978-1-56145-141-8 HC
ISBN 978-1-56145-174-6 PB

ISBN 978-1-56145-358-0 HC
ISBN 978-1-56145-407-5 PB

ISBN 978-1-56145-331-3 HC
ISBN 978-1-56145-406-8 PB

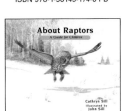

ISBN 978-1-56145-488-4 HC

ISBN 978-1-56145-536-2 HC

ISBN 978-1-56145-183-8 HC
ISBN 978-1-56145-233-0 PB

ISBN 978-1-56145-454-9 HC

ISBN 978-1-56145-588-1 HC

ABOUT HABITATS SERIES

ISBN 978-1-56145-390-0 HC   ISBN 978-1-56145-559-1 HC   ISBN 978-1-56145-469-3 HC   ISBN 978-1-56145-432-7 HC

THE SILLS

Cathryn Sill, a former elementary school teacher, is the author of the acclaimed ABOUT… series and ABOUT HABITATS series. With her husband John and her brother-in-law Ben Sill, she coauthored the popular bird-guide parodies, A FIELD GUIDE TO LITTLE-KNOWN AND SELDOM-SEEN BIRDS OF NORTH AMERICA, ANOTHER FIELD GUIDE TO LITTLE-KNOWN AND SELDOM-SEEN BIRDS OF NORTH AMERICA, and BEYOND BIRDWATCHING.

John Sill is a prize-winning and widely published wildlife artist who illustrated both the ABOUT… and ABOUT HABITATS series and illustrated and coauthored the FIELD GUIDES and BEYOND BIRDWATCHING. A native of North Carolina, he holds a B.S. in Wildlife Biology from North Carolina State University.

The Sills live in Franklin, North Carolina.